Cool SWEETS

& treats to eat

Easy Recipes for Kids to Cook

Lisa Wagner

ABDO
Publishing Company

TO ADULT HELPERS

You're invited to assist an up-and-coming chef in a kitchen near you! And it will pay off in many ways. Your children can develop new skills, gain confidence, and make some delicious food while learning to cook. What's more, it's going to be a lot of fun!

These recipes are designed to let children cook independently as much as possible. Encourage them to do whatever they are able to do on their own. Also encourage them to try the variations supplied with each recipe and to experiment with their own ideas. Building creativity into the cooking process encourages children to think like real chefs.

Before getting started, set some ground rules about using the kitchen, cooking tools, and ingredients. Most important, adult supervision is a must whenever a child uses the stove, oven, or sharp tools. (Look for the Hot Stuff! and Super Sharp! symbols.)

So, put on your aprons and stand by. Let your young chefs take the lead. Watch and learn. Taste their creations. Praise their efforts. Enjoy the culinary adventure!

Visit us at www.abdopublishing.com

Published by ABDO Publishing Company, 4940 Viking Drive, Edina, Minnesota 55435. Copyright © 2007 by Abdo Consulting Group, Inc. International copyrights reserved in all countries. No part of this book may be reproduced in any form without written permission from the publisher. The Checkerboard Library™ is a trademark and logo of ABDO Publishing Company.

Printed in the United States.

Design and Production: Mighty Media, Inc.
Art Direction: Anders Hanson
Photo Credits: Anders Hanson, Shutterstock
Series Editor: Pam Price

The following manufacturers/names appearing in this book are trademarks: Pyrex®, Chex®, Cheerios®, Jet Puffed® Marshmallow Cream, Reynolds® Cut-Rite® Waxed Paper, Target® Aluminum Foil, Anderson's® Pure Maple Syrup, Santini® Organic Syrup, Skippy® Peanut Butter, Old Home® Plain Yogurt, Lea & Perrins® Worcestershire Sauce, Morton® Iodized Salt

Library of Congress Cataloging-in-Publication Data

Wagner, Lisa, 1958-
  Cool sweets & treats to eat : easy recipes for kids to cook / Lisa Wagner.
    p. cm. -- (Cool cooking)
  Includes index.
  ISBN-13: 978-1-59928-726-3
  ISBN-10: 1-59928-726-9
  1. Snack foods--Juvenile literature. 2. Desserts--Juvenile literature. I. Title.
II. Title: Cool sweets and treats to eat.

  TX740.W2144 2007
  641.5'3--dc22

                                    2006032959

Table of Contents

What Makes Cooking So Cool

Welcome to the world of cooking! The cool thing about cooking is that you are the chef! You get to decide what to cook, how to cook, and what ingredients you want to use.

Everything you need to know to get started is in this book. You will learn the basic cooking terms and tools. All of the recipes in this book require only basic kitchen equipment. All the tools you will need are pictured on pages 8 through 9.

Most of the ingredients used in these recipes are shown on pages 12 through 15. This will help you identify the items for your grocery list. You want to find the freshest ingredients possible when shopping. You may notice some foods marked *organic*. This means that the food was grown using earth-friendly fertilizers and pest control methods.

This book is filled with recipes for tasty snacks and delicious treats. Most are quick and easy to prepare. You probably have many of the ingredients in your kitchen already. In fact, you might be surprised to discover how ordinary ingredients can be turned into amazing treats!

Most of the recipes have variations, so you can be creative. A recipe can be different every time you make it. Get inspired and give a recipe your original touch. Being a cook is like being an artist in the kitchen. The most important ingredient is imagination!

GET THE PICTURE!

When a step number in a recipe has a dotted circle around it, look for the picture that goes with it. The circle around the photo will be the same color as the step number.

4 →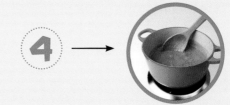

The Basics

Get going in the right direction with a few important basics!

ASK PERMISSION

> Before you cook, get permission to use the kitchen, cooking tools, and ingredients.

> If you'd like to do everything by yourself, say so. As long as you can do it safely, do it.

> When you need help, ask. Always get help when you use the stove or oven.

BE PREPARED

> Being well organized is a chef's secret ingredient for success!

> Read through the entire recipe before you do anything else.

> Gather all your cooking tools and ingredients.

> Get the ingredients ready. The list of ingredients tells how to prepare each item.

> Put each prepared ingredient into a separate bowl.

> Read the recipe instructions carefully. Do the steps in the order they are listed.

BE SMART, BE SAFE

> If you use the stove or oven, you need an adult in the kitchen with you.

> Never use the stove or oven if you are home alone!

> Always get an adult to help with the hot jobs, such as draining boiling water.

> Have an adult nearby when you are using a sharp tool such as a knife, peeler, or grater. Always use sharp tools with care.

> Always turn pot handles toward the back of the stove. This helps prevent you from accidentally knocking over pots.

> Prevent accidents by working slowly and carefully. Take your time.

> If you get hurt, let an adult know right away!

BE NEAT AND CLEAN

> Start with clean hands, clean tools, and a clean work surface.

> Tie back long hair so it stays out of the way and out of the food.

> Wear comfortable clothing and roll up your sleeves.

> Aprons and chef hats are optional!

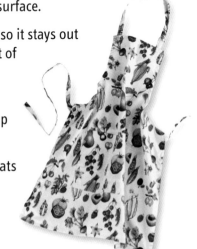

Make a Good Match!

Have fun and invent your own recipes by substituting one ingredient for another. Use the same amount of the substitute ingredient as the one it is replacing. The only thing you need to remember is to make a good match. It is best to make substitutions with dry ingredients, fruits, or vegetables. For example, if you prefer almonds or sunflower seeds to peanuts, go ahead and use them. If a recipe calls for raspberries, try using blueberries or strawberries instead. No carrots in the house? Try another crunchy vegetable such as celery, jicama, or green pepper.

MEASURING

Most ingredients are measured by the cup, tablespoon, or teaspoon.

Measuring cups and spoons come in a variety of sizes. An amount is printed or etched on each one to show how much it holds. To measure ½ cup, use the measuring cup marked ½ cup and fill it to the top.

Some measuring cups are large and have marks showing various amounts.

Ingredients such as meat and cheese are measured by weight in ounces or pounds. You purchase them by weight too.

KEY SYMBOLS

In this book, you will see some symbols beside the recipes. Here is what they mean.

HOT STUFF!

The recipe requires the use of a stove or oven. You need adult assistance and supervision.

SUPER SHARP!

A sharp tool such as a peeler, knife, or grater is needed. Get an adult to stand by.

EVEN COOLER!

This symbol means adventure! It could be a tip for making the recipe spicier. Sometimes it's a wild variation using an unusual ingredient. Give it a try! Get inspired and invent your own super-cool ideas.

TIP: Set a measuring cup inside a large bowl to catch spills. Hold a measuring spoon over a small bowl or cup to catch spills.

The Tool Box

A box on the bottom of the first page of each recipe lists the tools you need.
When you come across a tool you don't know, turn back to these pages.

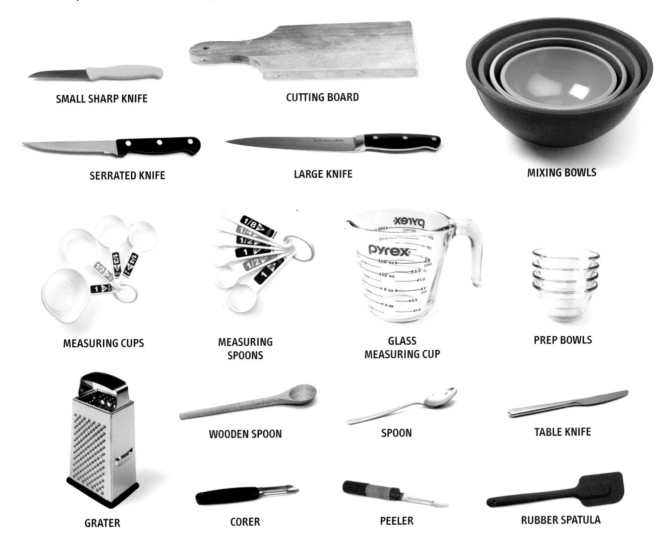

SMALL SHARP KNIFE

CUTTING BOARD

MIXING BOWLS

SERRATED KNIFE

LARGE KNIFE

MEASURING CUPS

MEASURING
SPOONS

GLASS
MEASURING CUP

PREP BOWLS

GRATER

WOODEN SPOON

SPOON

TABLE KNIFE

CORER

PEELER

RUBBER SPATULA

JUICER

STRAINER

BAKING SHEET

SAUCEPAN

WOODEN CRAFT STICKS

OVEN-SAFE PLATTER

MICROWAVE-SAFE PLATE

8 × 8 BAKING PAN

TIMER

MICROWAVE OVEN

9 × 13 BAKING PAN

PAPER TOWELS

TOWELS

POT HOLDER

WAXED PAPER CUPS

ALUMINUM FOIL

WAXED PAPER

BAKING PARCHMENT

Cool Cooking Terms

You need to learn the basic cooking terms and the actions that go with them. Whenever you need to remind yourself, just turn back to these pages.

Most ingredients need preparation before they are cooked or assembled. Look at the list of ingredients beside the recipe. After some items, you'll see words such as *chopped*, *sliced*, or *diced*. These words tell you how to prepare the ingredients.

FIRST THINGS FIRST

Always wash fruit and vegetables well. Rinse them under cold water. Pat them dry with a towel. Then they won't slip so easily when you cut them.

CHOP

Chop means to cut things into small pieces. The more you chop, the smaller the pieces. If a recipe says finely chopped, it means you need very small pieces.

PEEL

Peel means to remove the skin. Use a peeler for carrots, potatoes, cucumbers, and apples. Hold the item to be peeled against the cutting board. Slide the peeler away from you along the surface of the food.

TIP: To peel onion or garlic, remove the papery shell. Trim each end with a sharp knife. Then peel off the outer layer with your fingers. Never put garlic or onion peels in a food disposer!

MINCE

Mince means to cut the food into the tiniest possible pieces. Garlic is often minced and sometimes onion is too.

SLICE

Slice means to cut food into pieces of the same thickness.

SPREAD

Spread means to smooth an ingredient across a surface. Use a knife or a rubber spatula to spread creamy ingredients into a smooth, even layer.

FOLD

Fold means to gently mix ingredients together. Use a rubber spatula or a spoon to lift and turn the mixture just until it is blended. Don't overdo it!

GRATE

Grate means to shred something into small pieces using a grater. A grater has surfaces covered in holes with raised, sharp edges. You rub the food against a surface using firm pressure.

MIX

When you mix, you stir ingredients together, usually with a large spoon. *Blend* is another word for *mix*.

CORE

Core means to remove the core and seeds from a fruit, usually an apple. Use a special tool called a corer to make this job easier. Put a clean apple on a cutting board and center the

corer over the middle of it. Press the corer all the way through the apple until it hits the cutting board. Twist the corer to loosen the core and seeds. Then pull the corer back out of the apple. The core and seeds will come out of the apple when you pull out the corer.

GREASE

Grease means to coat a surface of a pan with oil or butter to keep food from sticking to it. Use a **wad** of waxed paper or paper towel to spread a light layer of grease evenly over the pan.

The Coolest Ingredients

GREEN PEPPER

BABY CARROTS

CARROTS

BROCCOLI

JICAMA

CUCUMBER

CAULIFLOWER

CELERY

WHITE ONION

TOMATO

GRANNY SMITH APPLE

RASPBERRIES

STRAWBERRIES

DRIED APRICOTS

LEMON

LIMES

TORTILLA CHIPS

PRETZELS

CORN CHEX CEREAL

WHEAT CHEX CEREAL

CHEERIOS

GRAHAM CRACKERS

FLOUR

SUGAR

BROWN SUGAR

MAPLE SYRUP

RASPBERRY SYRUP

PEANUT BUTTER

SCALLIONS

CILANTRO

CHEDDAR CHEESE

BUTTER

13

Allergy Alert

Some people have a reaction when they eat certain kinds of food. If you have any allergies, you know what it's all about. An allergic reaction can require emergency medical help. Nut allergies are serious and can be especially dangerous. Before you serve anything made with nuts, ask if anyone has a nut allergy. People with nut allergies will not be able to eat what you have prepared. Don't be offended. It might save a life!

SOUR CREAM

YOGURT

RASPBERRY YOGURT

ROLLED OATS

SUNFLOWER SEEDS

SESAME SEEDS

FLAKED COCONUT

CASHEWS

PEANUTS

SEMI-SWEET CHOCOLATE CHIPS

WHITE CHOCOLATE CHIPS

CHOCOLATE CANDY BAR

MARSHMALLOW CREAM **OLIVE OIL** **WORCESTERSHIRE SAUCE** **SALT**

ONION POWDER **CHILI POWDER** **CINNAMON** **GARLIC POWDER** **DRIED DILL WEED**

Get Fresh!

Dried herbs are stronger than fresh herbs. If you substitute fresh herbs for dried herbs, use at least three times as much as the recipe calls for. For example, if the recipe says 1 teaspoon of dried basil, use 3 teaspoons of chopped fresh basil.

Dilly & Chilly Dips for Veggies

What the best-dressed veggies are wearing!

MAKES 2 CUPS

INGREDIENTS

FOR DILLY DIP

1 cup sour cream

1 cup plain yogurt

¼ cup minced white onion

2 teaspoons dried dill weed

½ teaspoon salt

FOR CHILLY DIP

1 cup sour cream

1 cup plain yogurt

4 scallions, chopped

1½ teaspoons chili powder

½ teaspoon garlic powder

½ teaspoon salt

TOOLS:	Cutting board	Measuring cups	Spoon
	Small sharp knife	Prep bowls	
	Measuring spoons	Small mixing bowls	

1 To make either dip, mix all the ingredients together until they are well blended.

2 Put the dip in a bowl and place it on a serving platter. Surround the bowl of dip with vegetables.

Variations

> Serve the dip in a veggie! Cut a green or a red pepper in half and remove the seeds. Set the pepper on a serving plate and fill the cavity with dip.

> For a thicker dip, use only sour cream instead of a yogurt and sour cream mixture.

Even Cooler!

> If you like your dip more dilly, add another teaspoon of dill weed.

> For extra chilly dip, add another teaspoon of chili powder.

SUGGESTED VEGGIES

Carrots, peeled and cut in 3-inch pieces	Green pepper, cut in strips	Cucumber, peeled and sliced in ½-inch rounds
Baby carrots	Cauliflower, cut in bite-size pieces	Jicama, peeled and cut in 3-inch strips
Celery, cut in 3-inch pieces	Broccoli, cut in bite-size pieces	

Nachos with Pico de Gallo

Chips and cheese with a sidekick!

SERVES 4

INGREDIENTS

FOR PICO DE GALLO

2 large tomatoes, chopped (about 2 cups)

½ cup chopped white onion

¼ cup chopped fresh cilantro

Juice squeezed from ½ lime

1 teaspoon olive oil

½ teaspoon salt

FOR NACHOS

8 ounces tortilla chips (about half a large bag)

3 cups grated Cheddar cheese

TOOLS: Cutting board
Serrated knife
Small sharp knife
Grater

Measuring spoons
Measuring cups
Prep bowls
Small mixing bowl

Spoon
Oven-safe platter

1 Preheat the oven to 400 degrees.

2 Mix the tomatoes, white onion, cilantro, lime juice, olive oil, and salt together in small mixing bowl. Cover and set it aside.

3 Put the chips on an oven-safe platter and sprinkle the cheese evenly over them.

4 Put the platter in the oven and bake for 5 minutes, or until the cheese is bubbling.

5 Let the nachos cool slightly before serving them. Be careful, the platter will still be hot!

6 Serve with the pico de gallo.

Variations

> For speedy nachos (and no hot platter), use a microwave oven to melt the cheese. Start with 1 minute on high power. Then turn the platter to help the cheese melt evenly. Continue to cook in 30-second **increments** until the cheese is melted.

> Create your own nachos with different toppings. Try chopped scallions, chopped black olives, diced tomatoes, diced cooked chicken, refried beans, or taco meat.

No-Bake Energy Bars

A nutritious and delicious
energy boost in a bar!

MAKES 24 BARS

INGREDIENTS

Butter or oil for greasing the pan
1 cup semi-sweet chocolate chips
1½ cups rolled oats
2 cups crisp rice cereal
½ cup flaked coconut
½ cup sesame seeds
1 cup sunflower seeds
¾ cup peanut butter
¾ cup brown sugar
¾ cup maple syrup

TOOLS:

9 × 13 pan	Saucepan	Spoon
Waxed paper	Wooden spoon	Large knife
Measuring cups	Prep bowls	
Rubber spatula	Large mixing bowl	

1. Lightly grease the bottom and sides of the baking pan with a small amount of butter or oil. Use a **wad** of waxed paper to spread the butter or oil.

2. Put the chocolate chips, oats, crisp rice cereal, coconut, sesame seeds, and sunflower seeds in a large mixing bowl and mix them together.

3. Put the peanut butter, brown sugar, and maple syrup in a saucepan. Use a rubber spatula to help get the peanut butter in and out of the measuring cup.

4. Place the saucepan over medium heat and stir with a wooden spoon. Continue to stir until everything is blended and the brown sugar has dissolved.

5. Pour the hot mixture over the dry ingredients in the mixing bowl and stir. Keep stirring until everything is completely blended.

6. Pour the mixture into the prepared baking pan. Use your clean hands to firmly pat the mixture into the pan.

7. Refrigerate for at least 3 hours, then use a large knife to cut the bars. These will be solid and difficult to cut, so ask for help.

··· Variations ···

> Use raisins instead of coconut.

> Substitute chopped peanuts or almonds for the sunflower seeds.

> Try butterscotch chips instead of semi-sweet chocolate chips.

Even Cooler!

To make this snack extra **nutritious**, add ½ cup of wheat germ to the mixture.

Super Cereal Snack Mix

Cereal makes a snack-time appearance!

MAKES 9 CUPS

TOOLS: Measuring cups Wooden spoon
Measuring spoons 9 × 13 pan
Mixing bowl Aluminum foil

22

1 Preheat the oven to 250 degrees.

2 Mix the pretzels, nuts, and cereals together in a large mixing bowl.

3 Put the butter in the baking pan and place it in the oven to melt the butter. This takes about 10 minutes.

4 Remove the pan from the oven and add the Worcestershire sauce, garlic powder, and onion powder. Stir to mix.

5 Add the ingredients from the mixing bowl to the baking pan. Gently stir until everything is coated with the butter mixture.

6 Return the pan to the oven and bake for 50 to 60 minutes. Stir every 10 minutes. The mix is done when it is crisp and golden brown.

7 While the mix is baking, cover a flat surface with aluminum foil.

8 When the mix is done, pour it onto the foil and let it cool.

Variations

> Use different kinds of nuts in place of the cashew pieces and peanuts. Sunflower seeds, almonds, and pecans are tasty alternatives.

> Add 1 teaspoon of seasoned salt to the butter mixture.

Berry Frozen Fruit Pops

INGREDIENTS

1½ cups raspberry yogurt
2 tablespoons raspberry syrup
1 cup fresh raspberries

Berry,
berry
delicious.
And good
for you!

MAKES 4
FRUIT POPS

TOOLS: Measuring cups
Measuring spoons
Small mixing bowl
4 5-ounce waxed
paper cups
4 wooden craft sticks

24

1. Mix the yogurt and syrup together until they are blended. Gently fold in the raspberries.

2. Distribute the mixture evenly into the paper cups. Put a wooden craft stick in the middle of each cup.

3. Place the cups in the freezer for 6 to 8 hours. If you make these in the evening, they will be ready for after-school snacking the next day.

4. Tear the paper cup away from the frozen pop and enjoy!

Even Cooler!

Make **two-tone** berry pops. Make a raspberry yogurt mixture and a blueberry yogurt mixture. Distribute either mixture evenly among 8 waxed paper cups, filling each cup about halfway. Then finish filling the cups with the other mixture. Put in the sticks and freeze as in step 3 above. This cool alternative makes 8 pops.

Variations

> For blueberry pops, use blueberry yogurt, blueberry syrup, and fresh blueberries.

> Make maple-vanilla pops with vanilla yogurt, maple syrup, and vanilla-coated raisins.

Over-the-Top Apple Crisp

A heap of apples under a topping of crunchy sweetness!

MAKES 6 SERVINGS

INGREDIENTS

5 or 6 large Granny Smith apples (about 2 pounds), peeled, cored, and thinly sliced

Juice of ½ lemon

¼ cup water

½ cup sugar

½ cup brown sugar

1 teaspoon cinnamon

¼ teaspoon salt

¾ cup flour

1 stick butter, cut into 8 pieces

TOOLS: 8 × 8 baking pan
Peeler
Corer
Small sharp knife

Juicer
Strainer
Measuring cups
Measuring spoons

Large mixing bowl
Aluminum foil

1 Preheat the oven to 350 degrees.

2 Put the sliced apples in the baking pan. They might be higher than the top of the pan. Don't worry, they will shrink as they bake.

3 Strain the lemon juice and mix it with the water. Pour the mixture evenly over the apples.

4 Put the rest of the ingredients in a large mixing bowl. Use your clean hands to rub the butter into the dry ingredients.

5 Sprinkle the mixture evenly over the apples but don't mix the two together.

6 Cover the pan loosely with aluminum foil and put it in the oven. Bake for 25 minutes and then remove the foil. Bake for another 35 minutes, or until the topping is golden brown.

Even Cooler!

Serve warm pieces of apple crisp with vanilla or cinnamon ice cream on the side.

Chocolate-Dipped Treats

Elegant treats you make in minutes!

INGREDIENTS

12 strawberries

12 dried apricots

24 small pretzel twists

1 cup semi-sweet chocolate chips

1 cup white chocolate chips

MAKES 24 FRUIT PIECES
AND 24 PRETZEL PIECES

TOOLS: Paper towels
Waxed paper or baking parchment
Baking sheet
Glass measuring cup
Microwave oven
Spoon

CHOCOLATE-DIPPED FRUIT

1 Wash the strawberries and the apricots. Dry them well with paper towels. The fruit needs to be very dry so the chocolate will stick to it. Leave the stems on the strawberries so you can hold the stem while you dip the strawberry. Also, it is pretty to see the green stem on the red berry!

2 Cover a baking sheet with a piece of waxed paper or baking parchment.

3 Put the semi-sweet chocolate chips in a glass measuring cup. Microwave them on high power for 60 seconds. Stir the chips to help them melt.

4 Return the chips to the microwave for another 30 seconds. Remove them and stir them again. Continue doing this until the chips are completely melted.

5 Hold a strawberry by the stem and dip it into the chocolate. Leave a little bit of the red berry showing above the chocolate.

6 Place the strawberry on the covered baking pan. Continue to dip the rest of the strawberries and then dip the apricots. Dip the apricots about halfway into the chocolate.

7 Put the baking pan in the refrigerator for about 15 minutes, or until the chocolate hardens.

CHOCOLATE-DIPPED PRETZELS

1 Begin with step 2 above. Use the same **technique**, but substitute white chocolate chips for the semi-sweet chocolate chips.

TIP: The pretzels and apricots will stay fresh for a week in sealed plastic bags. Store them away from heat or in the refrigerator. The chocolate-dipped strawberries should be eaten the same day you make them.

Campfire-Free S'mores

Classic camping treats to make at home!

MAKES 8 S'MORES

1 Break the graham crackers in half. Spread 1 tablespoon of marshmallow cream on 8 of the cracker halves. Break each chocolate bar into 4 pieces. Put 1 piece of chocolate on each of the other 8 cracker halves.

2 Put 2 crackers with chocolate on a microwave-safe plate. Microwave on high power for 30 seconds. The chocolate should be soft but not melted. Repeat this step with the other 6 cracker halves with chocolate on them.

3 Place a marshmallow-coated cracker half on top of each cracker with chocolate.

TOOLS: Measuring spoons
Microwave-safe plate
Microwave oven

Important!

Do not make this recipe with regular marshmallows. When marshmallows are melted with a microwave oven, they get very sticky and can be a choking **hazard**.

Glossary

hazard – a source of danger.

increment – the amount by which something increases.

nutritious – providing the nutrients necessary for growth and health.

technique – a method or style in which something is done.

two-tone – having two colors or two shades of one color.

wad – a small ball or lump of material.

Web Sites

To learn more about cool cooking, visit ABDO Publishing Company on the World Wide Web at **www.abdopublishing.com**. Web sites about cool cooking are featured on our Book Links page. These links are routinely monitored and updated to provide the most current information available.

Index